ASA-SP-INK

THE STANDARD® PILOT LOG
SP-INK

ASA-SP-INK
ISBN 978-1-61954-277-8

Printed in Turkey

Aviation Supplies & Academics, Inc.
7005 132nd Place SE
Newcastle, Washington 98059 USA
asa2fly.com | asa@asa2fly.com

TRANSPORTATION USD $15.95

ISBN 978-1-61954-277-8
51595 >
9 781619 542778

The Standard Pilot Log

Name ______________________ **Logbook Number** ____________

Mailing Address ______________________ **From** ____________

______________________ **To** ____________

Certificates Held

Type	Date Issued	Certificate Number
REMOTE PILOT		
STUDENT PILOT		
SPORT PILOT		
RECREATIONAL PILOT		
PRIVATE PILOT		
COMMERCIAL PILOT		
FLIGHT INSTRUCTOR		
IRLINE TRANSPORT PILOT		
VIATION MECHANIC		
GROUND INSTRUCTOR		

Rating Record

☐ AIRPLANE ☐ INSTRUMENT ☐ UNMANNED (UAS)

☐ SINGLE ENGINE: ☐ LAND ☐ SEA

☐ MULTI-ENGINE: ☐ LAND ☐ SEA

☐ MULTI-ENGINE: Limited to Center Line Thrust

☐ GLIDER ☐ AERO TOW ☐ WINCH TOW

☐ POWERED PARACHUTE ☐ WEIGHT-SHIFT CONTROL

☐ ROTORCRAFT ☐ HELICOPTER ☐ GYROPLANE

☐ LIGHTER-THAN-AIR ☐ AIRSHIP ☐ BALLOON

☐ POWERED LIFT

☐ GI BASIC ☐ GI ADVANCED ☐ GI INSTRUMENT

☐ OTHER RATINGS (Specify) ____________

Aircraft Type Ratings

____

YEAR 20___ DATE	AIRCRAFT MAKE & MODEL	AIRCRAFT IDENT.	POINTS OF DEPARTURE & ARRIVAL		AIRCRAFT CATEGORY			GROUND TRAINER	TYPE OF PILOTING TIME		
			FROM	TO	AIRPLANE **SEL**	AIRPLANE **MEL**			DUAL RECEIVED	PILOT-IN-COMMAND	
				PAGE TOTAL							
				AMOUNT FORWARD							
				TOTAL TO DATE							

CONDITIONS OF FLIGHT					NO. INSTR. APPR.	NO. LDG. DAY / NIGHT	TOTAL DURATION OF FLIGHT	REMARKS, PROCEDURES, MANEUVERS
DAY	NIGHT	CROSS-COUNTRY	ACTUAL INSTR.	SIMULATED INSTR.				

I certify that the statements made by me on this form are true.

PILOT'S SIGNATURE

YEAR 20___			POINTS OF DEPARTURE & ARRIVAL		AIRCRAFT CATEGORY				TYPE OF PILOTING TIME		
DATE	AIRCRAFT MAKE & MODEL	AIRCRAFT IDENT.	FROM	TO	AIRPLANE **SEL**	AIRPLANE **MEL**		GROUND TRAINER	DUAL RECEIVED	PILOT-IN-COMMAND	
				PAGE TOTAL							
				AMOUNT FORWARD							
				TOTAL TO DATE							

CONDITIONS OF FLIGHT										NO. INSTR. APPR.	NO. LDG. DAY / NIGHT	TOTAL DURATION OF FLIGHT		REMARKS, PROCEDURES, MANEUVERS
DAY		NIGHT		CROSS-COUNTRY		ACTUAL INSTR.		SIMULATED INSTR.						

I certify that the statements made by me on this form are true.

PILOT'S SIGNATURE

YEAR 20___ DATE	AIRCRAFT MAKE & MODEL	AIRCRAFT IDENT.	POINTS OF DEPARTURE & ARRIVAL		AIRCRAFT CATEGORY			GROUND TRAINER	TYPE OF PILOTING TIME		
			FROM	TO	AIRPLANE **SEL**	AIRPLANE **MEL**			DUAL RECEIVED	PILOT-IN-COMMAND	
				PAGE TOTAL							
				AMOUNT FORWARD							
				TOTAL TO DATE							

CONDITIONS OF FLIGHT					NO. INSTR. APPR.	NO. LDG. DAY / NIGHT	TOTAL DURATION OF FLIGHT	REMARKS, PROCEDURES, MANEUVERS
DAY	NIGHT	CROSS-COUNTRY	ACTUAL INSTR.	SIMULATED INSTR.				

I certify that the statements made by me on this form are true.

PILOT'S SIGNATURE

YEAR 20___			POINTS OF DEPARTURE & ARRIVAL		AIRCRAFT CATEGORY				TYPE OF PILOTING TIME		
DATE	AIRCRAFT MAKE & MODEL	AIRCRAFT IDENT.	FROM	TO	AIRPLANE **SEL**	AIRPLANE **MEL**		GROUND TRAINER	DUAL RECEIVED	PILOT-IN-COMMAND	
				PAGE TOTAL							
				AMOUNT FORWARD							
				TOTAL TO DATE							

CONDITIONS OF FLIGHT										NO. INSTR. APPR.	NO. LDG. DAY / NIGHT	TOTAL DURATION OF FLIGHT		REMARKS, PROCEDURES, MANEUVERS
DAY		NIGHT		CROSS-COUNTRY		ACTUAL INSTR.		SIMULATED INSTR.						

I certify that the statements made by me on this form are true.

PILOT'S SIGNATURE

YEAR 20___ DATE	AIRCRAFT MAKE & MODEL	AIRCRAFT IDENT.	POINTS OF DEPARTURE & ARRIVAL		AIRCRAFT CATEGORY			GROUND TRAINER	TYPE OF PILOTING TIME		
			FROM	TO	AIRPLANE **SEL**	AIRPLANE **MEL**			DUAL RECEIVED	PILOT-IN-COMMAND	
				PAGE TOTAL							
				AMOUNT FORWARD							
				TOTAL TO DATE							

CONDITIONS OF FLIGHT					NO. INSTR. APPR.	NO. LDG. DAY / NIGHT	TOTAL DURATION OF FLIGHT	REMARKS, PROCEDURES, MANEUVERS
DAY	NIGHT	CROSS-COUNTRY	ACTUAL INSTR.	SIMULATED INSTR.				

I certify that tho statements made by me on this form are true.

PILOT'S SIGNATURE

YEAR 20___ DATE	AIRCRAFT MAKE & MODEL	AIRCRAFT IDENT.	POINTS OF DEPARTURE & ARRIVAL		AIRCRAFT CATEGORY			GROUND TRAINER	TYPE OF PILOTING TIME		
			FROM	TO	AIRPLANE **SEL**	AIRPLANE **MEL**			DUAL RECEIVED	PILOT-IN-COMMAND	
				PAGE TOTAL							
				AMOUNT FORWARD							
				TOTAL TO DATE							

CONDITIONS OF FLIGHT					NO. INSTR. APPR.	NO. LDG. DAY / NIGHT	TOTAL DURATION OF FLIGHT	REMARKS, PROCEDURES, MANEUVERS
DAY	NIGHT	CROSS-COUNTRY	ACTUAL INSTR.	SIMULATED INSTR.				

I certify that tho statements made by me on this form are true.

PILOT'S SIGNATURE

YEAR 20___ DATE	AIRCRAFT MAKE & MODEL	AIRCRAFT IDENT.	POINTS OF DEPARTURE & ARRIVAL		AIRCRAFT CATEGORY			GROUND TRAINER	TYPE OF PILOTING TIME		
			FROM	TO	AIRPLANE **SEL**	AIRPLANE **MEL**			DUAL RECEIVED	PILOT-IN-COMMAND	
				PAGE TOTAL							
				AMOUNT FORWARD							
				TOTAL TO DATE							

CONDITIONS OF FLIGHT										NO. INSTR. APPR.	NO. LDG. DAY / NIGHT	TOTAL DURATION OF FLIGHT		REMARKS, PROCEDURES, MANEUVERS
DAY		NIGHT		CROSS-COUNTRY		ACTUAL INSTR.		SIMULATED INSTR.						

I certify that the statements made by me on this form are true.

PILOT'S SIGNATURE

YEAR 20___			POINTS OF DEPARTURE & ARRIVAL		AIRCRAFT CATEGORY				TYPE OF PILOTING TIME		
DATE	AIRCRAFT MAKE & MODEL	AIRCRAFT IDENT.	FROM	TO	AIRPLANE **SEL**	AIRPLANE **MEL**		GROUND TRAINER	DUAL RECEIVED	PILOT-IN-COMMAND	
				PAGE TOTAL							
				AMOUNT FORWARD							
				TOTAL TO DATE							

CONDITIONS OF FLIGHT										NO. INSTR. APPR.	NO. LDG. DAY / NIGHT	TOTAL DURATION OF FLIGHT		REMARKS, PROCEDURES, MANEUVERS
DAY		NIGHT		CROSS-COUNTRY		ACTUAL INSTR.		SIMULATED INSTR.						

I certify that the statements made by me on this form are true.

PILOT'S SIGNATURE

YEAR 20___			POINTS OF DEPARTURE & ARRIVAL		AIRCRAFT CATEGORY				TYPE OF PILOTING TIME		
DATE	AIRCRAFT MAKE & MODEL	AIRCRAFT IDENT.	FROM	TO	AIRPLANE **SEL**	AIRPLANE **MEL**		GROUND TRAINER	DUAL RECEIVED	PILOT-IN-COMMAND	
				PAGE TOTAL							
				AMOUNT FORWARD							
				TOTAL TO DATE							

CONDITIONS OF FLIGHT					NO. INSTR. APPR.	NO. LDG. DAY / NIGHT	TOTAL DURATION OF FLIGHT	REMARKS, PROCEDURES, MANEUVERS
DAY	NIGHT	CROSS-COUNTRY	ACTUAL INSTR.	SIMULATED INSTR.				

I certify that the statements made by me on this form are true.

PILOT'S SIGNATURE

YEAR 20___ DATE	AIRCRAFT MAKE & MODEL	AIRCRAFT IDENT.	POINTS OF DEPARTURE & ARRIVAL		AIRCRAFT CATEGORY			GROUND TRAINER	TYPE OF PILOTING TIME		
			FROM	TO	AIRPLANE **SEL**	AIRPLANE **MEL**			DUAL RECEIVED	PILOT-IN-COMMAND	
				PAGE TOTAL							
				AMOUNT FORWARD							
				TOTAL TO DATE							

CONDITIONS OF FLIGHT					NO. INSTR. APPR.	NO. LDG. DAY / NIGHT	TOTAL DURATION OF FLIGHT	REMARKS, PROCEDURES, MANEUVERS
DAY	NIGHT	CROSS-COUNTRY	ACTUAL INSTR.	SIMULATED INSTR.				

I certify that the statements made by me on this form are true.

PILOT'S SIGNATURE

YEAR 20___ DATE	AIRCRAFT MAKE & MODEL	AIRCRAFT IDENT.	**POINTS OF DEPARTURE & ARRIVAL**		**AIRCRAFT CATEGORY**			GROUND TRAINER	**TYPE OF PILOTING TIME**		
			FROM	TO	AIRPLANE **SEL**	AIRPLANE **MEL**			DUAL RECEIVED	PILOT-IN-COMMAND	
				PAGE TOTAL							
				AMOUNT FORWARD							
				TOTAL TO DATE							

CONDITIONS OF FLIGHT										NO. INSTR. APPR.	NO. LDG. DAY / NIGHT	TOTAL DURATION OF FLIGHT		REMARKS, PROCEDURES, MANEUVERS
DAY		NIGHT		CROSS-COUNTRY		ACTUAL INSTR.		SIMULATED INSTR.						

I certify that the statements made by me on this form are true.

PILOT'S SIGNATURE

YEAR 20___			POINTS OF DEPARTURE & ARRIVAL		AIRCRAFT CATEGORY				TYPE OF PILOTING TIME		
DATE	AIRCRAFT MAKE & MODEL	AIRCRAFT IDENT.	FROM	TO	AIRPLANE **SEL**	AIRPLANE **MEL**		GROUND TRAINER	DUAL RECEIVED	PILOT-IN-COMMAND	
				PAGE TOTAL							
				AMOUNT FORWARD							
				TOTAL TO DATE							

CONDITIONS OF FLIGHT										NO. INSTR. APPR.	NO. LDG.	TOTAL DURATION OF FLIGHT		REMARKS, PROCEDURES, MANEUVERS
DAY		NIGHT		CROSS-COUNTRY		ACTUAL INSTR.		SIMULATED INSTR.			DAY / NIGHT			

I certify that the statements made by me on this form are true.

PILOT'S SIGNATURE

YEAR 20___ DATE	AIRCRAFT MAKE & MODEL	AIRCRAFT IDENT.	POINTS OF DEPARTURE & ARRIVAL		AIRCRAFT CATEGORY			GROUND TRAINER	TYPE OF PILOTING TIME		
			FROM	TO	AIRPLANE **SEL**	AIRPLANE **MEL**			DUAL RECEIVED	PILOT-IN-COMMAND	
				PAGE TOTAL							
				AMOUNT FORWARD							
				TOTAL TO DATE							

CONDITIONS OF FLIGHT					NO. INSTR. APPR.	NO. LDG. DAY / NIGHT	TOTAL DURATION OF FLIGHT	REMARKS, PROCEDURES, MANEUVERS
DAY	NIGHT	CROSS-COUNTRY	ACTUAL INSTR.	SIMULATED INSTR.				

I certify that the statements made by me on this form are true.

PILOT'S SIGNATURE

YEAR 20___ DATE	AIRCRAFT MAKE & MODEL	AIRCRAFT IDENT.	POINTS OF DEPARTURE & ARRIVAL		AIRCRAFT CATEGORY			GROUND TRAINER	TYPE OF PILOTING TIME		
			FROM	TO	AIRPLANE **SEL**	AIRPLANE **MEL**			DUAL RECEIVED	PILOT-IN-COMMAND	
				PAGE TOTAL							
				AMOUNT FORWARD							
				TOTAL TO DATE							

CONDITIONS OF FLIGHT					NO. INSTR. APPR.	NO. LDG. DAY / NIGHT	TOTAL DURATION OF FLIGHT	REMARKS, PROCEDURES, MANEUVERS
DAY	NIGHT	CROSS-COUNTRY	ACTUAL INSTR.	SIMULATED INSTR.				

I certify that the statements made by me on this form are true.

PILOT'S SIGNATURE

YEAR 20___ DATE	AIRCRAFT MAKE & MODEL	AIRCRAFT IDENT.	POINTS OF DEPARTURE & ARRIVAL		AIRCRAFT CATEGORY			GROUND TRAINER	TYPE OF PILOTING TIME		
			FROM	TO	AIRPLANE **SEL**	AIRPLANE **MEL**			DUAL RECEIVED	PILOT-IN-COMMAND	
				PAGE TOTAL							
				AMOUNT FORWARD							
				TOTAL TO DATE							

CONDITIONS OF FLIGHT					NO. INSTR. APPR.	NO. LDG. DAY / NIGHT	TOTAL DURATION OF FLIGHT	REMARKS, PROCEDURES, MANEUVERS
DAY	NIGHT	CROSS-COUNTRY	ACTUAL INSTR.	SIMULATED INSTR.				
								I certify that the statements made by me on this form are true.
								PILOT'S SIGNATURE

YEAR 20___ DATE	AIRCRAFT MAKE & MODEL	AIRCRAFT IDENT.	POINTS OF DEPARTURE & ARRIVAL		AIRCRAFT CATEGORY			GROUND TRAINER	TYPE OF PILOTING TIME		
			FROM	TO	AIRPLANE **SEL**	AIRPLANE **MEL**			DUAL RECEIVED	PILOT-IN-COMMAND	
				PAGE TOTAL							
				AMOUNT FORWARD							
				TOTAL TO DATE							

CONDITIONS OF FLIGHT										NO. INSTR. APPR.	NO. LDG. DAY / NIGHT	TOTAL DURATION OF FLIGHT		REMARKS, PROCEDURES, MANEUVERS
DAY		NIGHT		CROSS-COUNTRY		ACTUAL INSTR.		SIMULATED INSTR.						

I certify that the statements made by me on this form are true.

PILOT'S SIGNATURE

YEAR 20___ DATE	AIRCRAFT MAKE & MODEL	AIRCRAFT IDENT.	POINTS OF DEPARTURE & ARRIVAL		AIRCRAFT CATEGORY			GROUND TRAINER	TYPE OF PILOTING TIME		
			FROM	TO	AIRPLANE **SEL**	AIRPLANE **MEL**			DUAL RECEIVED	PILOT-IN-COMMAND	
				PAGE TOTAL							
				AMOUNT FORWARD							
				TOTAL TO DATE							

CONDITIONS OF FLIGHT					NO. INSTR. APPR.	NO. LDG. DAY / NIGHT	TOTAL DURATION OF FLIGHT	REMARKS, PROCEDURES, MANEUVERS
DAY	NIGHT	CROSS-COUNTRY	ACTUAL INSTR.	SIMULATED INSTR.				

I certify that the statements made by me on this form are true.

PILOT'S SIGNATURE

YEAR 20___ DATE	AIRCRAFT MAKE & MODEL	AIRCRAFT IDENT.	POINTS OF DEPARTURE & ARRIVAL		AIRCRAFT CATEGORY			GROUND TRAINER	TYPE OF PILOTING TIME		
			FROM	TO	AIRPLANE **SEL**	AIRPLANE **MEL**			DUAL RECEIVED	PILOT-IN-COMMAND	
				PAGE TOTAL							
				AMOUNT FORWARD							
				TOTAL TO DATE							

CONDITIONS OF FLIGHT					NO. INSTR. APPR.	NO. LDG.	TOTAL DURATION OF FLIGHT	REMARKS, PROCEDURES, MANEUVERS
DAY	NIGHT	CROSS-COUNTRY	ACTUAL INSTR.	SIMULATED INSTR.		DAY / NIGHT		

I certify that the statements made by me on this form are true.

PILOT'S SIGNATURE

YEAR 20___			POINTS OF DEPARTURE & ARRIVAL		AIRCRAFT CATEGORY				TYPE OF PILOTING TIME		
DATE	AIRCRAFT MAKE & MODEL	AIRCRAFT IDENT.	FROM	TO	AIRPLANE **SEL**	AIRPLANE **MEL**		GROUND TRAINER	DUAL RECEIVED	PILOT-IN-COMMAND	
				PAGE TOTAL							
				AMOUNT FORWARD							
				TOTAL TO DATE							

CONDITIONS OF FLIGHT					NO. INSTR. APPR.	NO. LDG. DAY / NIGHT	TOTAL DURATION OF FLIGHT	REMARKS, PROCEDURES, MANEUVERS
DAY	NIGHT	CROSS-COUNTRY	ACTUAL INSTR.	SIMULATED INSTR.				
								I certify that the statements made by me on this form are true.
								PILOT'S SIGNATURE

YEAR 20___			POINTS OF DEPARTURE & ARRIVAL		AIRCRAFT CATEGORY				TYPE OF PILOTING TIME		
DATE	AIRCRAFT MAKE & MODEL	AIRCRAFT IDENT.	FROM	TO	AIRPLANE **SEL**	AIRPLANE **MEL**		GROUND TRAINER	DUAL RECEIVED	PILOT-IN-COMMAND	
				PAGE TOTAL							
				AMOUNT FORWARD							
				TOTAL TO DATE							

CONDITIONS OF FLIGHT					NO. INSTR. APPR.	NO. LDG. DAY / NIGHT	TOTAL DURATION OF FLIGHT	REMARKS, PROCEDURES, MANEUVERS
DAY	NIGHT	CROSS-COUNTRY	ACTUAL INSTR.	SIMULATED INSTR.				
								I certify that the statements made by me on this form are true.
								PILOT'S SIGNATURE

YEAR 20___ DATE	AIRCRAFT MAKE & MODEL	AIRCRAFT IDENT.	**POINTS OF DEPARTURE & ARRIVAL**		**AIRCRAFT CATEGORY**			GROUND TRAINER	**TYPE OF PILOTING TIME**		
			FROM	TO	AIRPLANE **SEL**	AIRPLANE **MEL**			DUAL RECEIVED	PILOT-IN-COMMAND	
				PAGE TOTAL							
				AMOUNT FORWARD							
				TOTAL TO DATE							

CONDITIONS OF FLIGHT					NO. INSTR. APPR.	NO. LDG. DAY / NIGHT	TOTAL DURATION OF FLIGHT	REMARKS, PROCEDURES, MANEUVERS
DAY	NIGHT	CROSS-COUNTRY	ACTUAL INSTR.	SIMULATED INSTR.				

I certify that the statements made by me on this form are true.

PILOT'S SIGNATURE

YEAR 20___ DATE	AIRCRAFT MAKE & MODEL	AIRCRAFT IDENT.	POINTS OF DEPARTURE & ARRIVAL		AIRCRAFT CATEGORY			GROUND TRAINER	TYPE OF PILOTING TIME		
			FROM	TO	AIRPLANE **SEL**	AIRPLANE **MEL**			DUAL RECEIVED	PILOT-IN-COMMAND	
				PAGE TOTAL							
				AMOUNT FORWARD							
				TOTAL TO DATE							

CONDITIONS OF FLIGHT										NO. INSTR. APPR.	NO. LDG. DAY / NIGHT	TOTAL DURATION OF FLIGHT		REMARKS, PROCEDURES, MANEUVERS
DAY		NIGHT		CROSS-COUNTRY		ACTUAL INSTR.		SIMULATED INSTR.						
														I certify that the statements made by me on this form are true.
														PILOT'S SIGNATURE

YEAR 20___ DATE	AIRCRAFT MAKE & MODEL	AIRCRAFT IDENT.	POINTS OF DEPARTURE & ARRIVAL		AIRCRAFT CATEGORY			GROUND TRAINER	TYPE OF PILOTING TIME		
			FROM	TO	AIRPLANE **SEL**	AIRPLANE **MEL**			DUAL RECEIVED	PILOT-IN-COMMAND	
				PAGE TOTAL							
				AMOUNT FORWARD							
				TOTAL TO DATE							

CONDITIONS OF FLIGHT										NO. INSTR. APPR.	NO. LDG. DAY / NIGHT	TOTAL DURATION OF FLIGHT		REMARKS, PROCEDURES, MANEUVERS
DAY		NIGHT		CROSS-COUNTRY		ACTUAL INSTR.		SIMULATED INSTR.						

I certify that the statements made by me on this form are true.

PILOT'S SIGNATURE

YEAR 20___ DATE	AIRCRAFT MAKE & MODEL	AIRCRAFT IDENT.	POINTS OF DEPARTURE & ARRIVAL		AIRCRAFT CATEGORY			GROUND TRAINER	TYPE OF PILOTING TIME		
			FROM	TO	AIRPLANE **SEL**	AIRPLANE **MEL**			DUAL RECEIVED	PILOT-IN-COMMAND	
				PAGE TOTAL							
				AMOUNT FORWARD							
				TOTAL TO DATE							

CONDITIONS OF FLIGHT										NO. INSTR. APPR.	NO. LDG. DAY / NIGHT	TOTAL DURATION OF FLIGHT		REMARKS, PROCEDURES, MANEUVERS
DAY		NIGHT		CROSS-COUNTRY		ACTUAL INSTR.		SIMULATED INSTR.						

I certify that the statements made by me on this form are true.

PILOT'S SIGNATURE

YEAR 20___ DATE	AIRCRAFT MAKE & MODEL	AIRCRAFT IDENT.	POINTS OF DEPARTURE & ARRIVAL		AIRCRAFT CATEGORY			GROUND TRAINER	TYPE OF PILOTING TIME		
			FROM	TO	AIRPLANE **SEL**	AIRPLANE **MEL**			DUAL RECEIVED	PILOT-IN-COMMAND	
				PAGE TOTAL							
				AMOUNT FORWARD							
				TOTAL TO DATE							

CONDITIONS OF FLIGHT										NO. INSTR. APPR.	NO. LDG. DAY / NIGHT	TOTAL DURATION OF FLIGHT		REMARKS, PROCEDURES, MANEUVERS
DAY		NIGHT		CROSS-COUNTRY		ACTUAL INSTR.		SIMULATED INSTR.						
														I certify that the statements made by me on this form are true.
														PILOT'S SIGNATURE

YEAR 20___ DATE	AIRCRAFT MAKE & MODEL	AIRCRAFT IDENT.	POINTS OF DEPARTURE & ARRIVAL		AIRCRAFT CATEGORY			GROUND TRAINER	TYPE OF PILOTING TIME		
			FROM	TO	AIRPLANE **SEL**	AIRPLANE **MEL**			DUAL RECEIVED	PILOT-IN-COMMAND	
				PAGE TOTAL							
				AMOUNT FORWARD							
				TOTAL TO DATE							

CONDITIONS OF FLIGHT										NO. INSTR. APPR.	NO. LDG. DAY / NIGHT	TOTAL DURATION OF FLIGHT		REMARKS, PROCEDURES, MANEUVERS
DAY		NIGHT		CROSS-COUNTRY		ACTUAL INSTR.		SIMULATED INSTR.						

I certify that the statements made by me on this form are true.

PILOT'S SIGNATURE

YEAR 20___ DATE	AIRCRAFT MAKE & MODEL	AIRCRAFT IDENT.	POINTS OF DEPARTURE & ARRIVAL		AIRCRAFT CATEGORY						GROUND TRAINER		TYPE OF PILOTING TIME					
			FROM	TO	AIRPLANE **SEL**		AIRPLANE **MEL**						DUAL RECEIVED		PILOT-IN-COMMAND			
				PAGE TOTAL														
				AMOUNT FORWARD														
				TOTAL TO DATE														

CONDITIONS OF FLIGHT					NO. INSTR. APPR.	NO. LDG. DAY / NIGHT	TOTAL DURATION OF FLIGHT	REMARKS, PROCEDURES, MANEUVERS
DAY	NIGHT	CROSS-COUNTRY	ACTUAL INSTR.	SIMULATED INSTR.				

I certify that the statements made by me on this form are true.

PILOT'S SIGNATURE

YEAR 20___ DATE	AIRCRAFT MAKE & MODEL	AIRCRAFT IDENT.	POINTS OF DEPARTURE & ARRIVAL		AIRCRAFT CATEGORY			GROUND TRAINER	TYPE OF PILOTING TIME		
			FROM	TO	AIRPLANE **SEL**	AIRPLANE **MEL**			DUAL RECEIVED	PILOT-IN-COMMAND	
				PAGE TOTAL							
				AMOUNT FORWARD							
				TOTAL TO DATE							

CONDITIONS OF FLIGHT					NO. INSTR. APPR.	NO. LDG. DAY / NIGHT	TOTAL DURATION OF FLIGHT	REMARKS, PROCEDURES, MANEUVERS
DAY	NIGHT	CROSS-COUNTRY	ACTUAL INSTR.	SIMULATED INSTR.				

I certify that the statements made by me on this form are true

PILOT'S SIGNATURE

YEAR 20___ DATE	AIRCRAFT MAKE & MODEL	AIRCRAFT IDENT.	POINTS OF DEPARTURE & ARRIVAL		AIRCRAFT CATEGORY			GROUND TRAINER	TYPE OF PILOTING TIME		
			FROM	TO	AIRPLANE **SEL**	AIRPLANE **MEL**			DUAL RECEIVED	PILOT-IN-COMMAND	
				PAGE TOTAL							
				AMOUNT FORWARD							
				TOTAL TO DATE							

CONDITIONS OF FLIGHT					NO. INSTR. APPR.	NO. LDG. DAY / NIGHT	TOTAL DURATION OF FLIGHT	REMARKS, PROCEDURES, MANEUVERS
DAY	NIGHT	CROSS-COUNTRY	ACTUAL INSTR.	SIMULATED INSTR.				

								I certify that the statements made by me on this form are true.
								PILOT'S SIGNATURE

YEAR 20___			POINTS OF DEPARTURE & ARRIVAL		AIRCRAFT CATEGORY				TYPE OF PILOTING TIME		
DATE	AIRCRAFT MAKE & MODEL	AIRCRAFT IDENT.	FROM	TO	AIRPLANE **SEL**	AIRPLANE **MEL**		GROUND TRAINER	DUAL RECEIVED	PILOT-IN-COMMAND	
				PAGE TOTAL							
				AMOUNT FORWARD							
				TOTAL TO DATE							

CONDITIONS OF FLIGHT										NO. INSTR. APPR.	NO. LDG. DAY / NIGHT	TOTAL DURATION OF FLIGHT		REMARKS, PROCEDURES, MANEUVERS
DAY		NIGHT		CROSS-COUNTRY		ACTUAL INSTR.		SIMULATED INSTR.						

I certify that the statements made by me on this form are true.

PILOT'S SIGNATURE

YEAR 20___	AIRCRAFT MAKE & MODEL	AIRCRAFT IDENT.	POINTS OF DEPARTURE & ARRIVAL		AIRCRAFT CATEGORY			GROUND TRAINER	TYPE OF PILOTING TIME		
DATE			FROM	TO	AIRPLANE **SEL**	AIRPLANE **MEL**			DUAL RECEIVED	PILOT-IN-COMMAND	
				PAGE TOTAL							
				AMOUNT FORWARD							
				TOTAL TO DATE							

CONDITIONS OF FLIGHT										NO. INSTR. APPR.	NO. LDG. DAY/NIGHT	TOTAL DURATION OF FLIGHT		REMARKS, PROCEDURES, MANEUVERS
DAY		NIGHT		CROSS-COUNTRY		ACTUAL INSTR.		SIMULATED INSTR.						

I certify that the statements made by me on this form are true.

PILOT'S SIGNATURE

YEAR 20___			POINTS OF DEPARTURE & ARRIVAL		AIRCRAFT CATEGORY				TYPE OF PILOTING TIME		
DATE	AIRCRAFT MAKE & MODEL	AIRCRAFT IDENT.	FROM	TO	AIRPLANE **SEL**	AIRPLANE **MEL**		GROUND TRAINER	DUAL RECEIVED	PILOT-IN-COMMAND	
				PAGE TOTAL							
				AMOUNT FORWARD							
				TOTAL TO DATE							

CONDITIONS OF FLIGHT										NO. INSTR. APPR.	NO. LDG. DAY / NIGHT	TOTAL DURATION OF FLIGHT		REMARKS, PROCEDURES, MANEUVERS
DAY		NIGHT		CROSS-COUNTRY		ACTUAL INSTR.		SIMULATED INSTR.						

I certify that the statements made by me on this form are true.

PILOT'S SIGNATURE

YEAR 20___ DATE	AIRCRAFT MAKE & MODEL	AIRCRAFT IDENT.	POINTS OF DEPARTURE & ARRIVAL		AIRCRAFT CATEGORY			GROUND TRAINER	TYPE OF PILOTING TIME		
			FROM	TO	AIRPLANE **SEL**	AIRPLANE **MEL**			DUAL RECEIVED	PILOT-IN-COMMAND	
				PAGE TOTAL							
				AMOUNT FORWARD							
				TOTAL TO DATE							

CONDITIONS OF FLIGHT					NO. INSTR. APPR.	NO. LDG. DAY / NIGHT	TOTAL DURATION OF FLIGHT	REMARKS, PROCEDURES, MANEUVERS
DAY	NIGHT	CROSS-COUNTRY	ACTUAL INSTR.	SIMULATED INSTR.				

I certify that the statements made by me on this form are true.

PILOT'S SIGNATURE

YEAR 20___ DATE	AIRCRAFT MAKE & MODEL	AIRCRAFT IDENT.	POINTS OF DEPARTURE & ARRIVAL		AIRCRAFT CATEGORY			GROUND TRAINER	TYPE OF PILOTING TIME		
			FROM	TO	AIRPLANE **SEL**	AIRPLANE **MEL**			DUAL RECEIVED	PILOT-IN-COMMAND	
				PAGE TOTAL							
				AMOUNT FORWARD							
				TOTAL TO DATE							

CONDITIONS OF FLIGHT										NO. INSTR. APPR.	NO. LDG. DAY / NIGHT	TOTAL DURATION OF FLIGHT		REMARKS, PROCEDURES, MANEUVERS
DAY		NIGHT		CROSS-COUNTRY		ACTUAL INSTR.		SIMULATED INSTR.						

I certify that the statements made by me on this form are true.

PILOT'S SIGNATURE

YEAR 20___ DATE	AIRCRAFT MAKE & MODEL	AIRCRAFT IDENT.	POINTS OF DEPARTURE & ARRIVAL		AIRCRAFT CATEGORY			GROUND TRAINER	TYPE OF PILOTING TIME		
			FROM	TO	AIRPLANE **SEL**	AIRPLANE **MEL**			DUAL RECEIVED	PILOT-IN-COMMAND	
				PAGE TOTAL							
				AMOUNT FORWARD							
				TOTAL TO DATE							

CONDITIONS OF FLIGHT					NO. INSTR. APPR.	NO. LDG. DAY / NIGHT	TOTAL DURATION OF FLIGHT	REMARKS, PROCEDURES, MANEUVERS
DAY	NIGHT	CROSS-COUNTRY	ACTUAL INSTR.	SIMULATED INSTR.				

I certify that the statements made by me on this form are true.

PILOT'S SIGNATURE

YEAR 20___			POINTS OF DEPARTURE & ARRIVAL		AIRCRAFT CATEGORY				TYPE OF PILOTING TIME		
DATE	AIRCRAFT MAKE & MODEL	AIRCRAFT IDENT.	FROM	TO	AIRPLANE **SEL**	AIRPLANE **MEL**		GROUND TRAINER	DUAL RECEIVED	PILOT-IN-COMMAND	
				PAGE TOTAL							
				AMOUNT FORWARD							
				TOTAL TO DATE							

CONDITIONS OF FLIGHT					NO. INSTR. APPR.	NO. LDG. DAY / NIGHT	TOTAL DURATION OF FLIGHT	REMARKS, PROCEDURES, MANEUVERS
DAY	NIGHT	CROSS-COUNTRY	ACTUAL INSTR.	SIMULATED INSTR.				

I certify that the statements made by me on this form are true.

PILOT'S SIGNATURE

YEAR 20___ DATE	AIRCRAFT MAKE & MODEL	AIRCRAFT IDENT.	POINTS OF DEPARTURE & ARRIVAL		AIRCRAFT CATEGORY			GROUND TRAINER	TYPE OF PILOTING TIME		
			FROM	TO	AIRPLANE **SEL**	AIRPLANE **MEL**			DUAL RECEIVED	PILOT-IN-COMMAND	
				PAGE TOTAL							
				AMOUNT FORWARD							
				TOTAL TO DATE							

CONDITIONS OF FLIGHT					NO. INSTR. APPR.	NO. LDG. DAY / NIGHT	TOTAL DURATION OF FLIGHT	REMARKS, PROCEDURES, MANEUVERS
DAY	NIGHT	CROSS-COUNTRY	ACTUAL INSTR.	SIMULATED INSTR.				

I certify that the statements made by me on this form are true.

PILOT'S SIGNATURE

YEAR 20___ DATE	AIRCRAFT MAKE & MODEL	AIRCRAFT IDENT.	POINTS OF DEPARTURE & ARRIVAL		AIRCRAFT CATEGORY			GROUND TRAINER	TYPE OF PILOTING TIME		
			FROM	TO	AIRPLANE **SEL**	AIRPLANE **MEL**			DUAL RECEIVED	PILOT-IN-COMMAND	
				PAGE TOTAL							
				AMOUNT FORWARD							
				TOTAL TO DATE							

CONDITIONS OF FLIGHT										NO. INSTR. APPR.	NO. LDG. DAY / NIGHT	TOTAL DURATION OF FLIGHT		REMARKS, PROCEDURES, MANEUVERS
DAY		NIGHT		CROSS-COUNTRY		ACTUAL INSTR.		SIMULATED INSTR.						

I certify that the statements made by me on this form are true.

PILOT'S SIGNATURE

YEAR 20___ DATE	AIRCRAFT MAKE & MODEL	AIRCRAFT IDENT.	POINTS OF DEPARTURE & ARRIVAL		AIRCRAFT CATEGORY						GROUND TRAINER		TYPE OF PILOTING TIME					
			FROM	TO	AIRPLANE **SEL**		AIRPLANE **MEL**						DUAL RECEIVED		PILOT-IN-COMMAND			
				PAGE TOTAL														
				AMOUNT FORWARD														
				TOTAL TO DATE														

CONDITIONS OF FLIGHT					NO. INSTR. APPR.	NO. LDG. DAY / NIGHT	TOTAL DURATION OF FLIGHT	REMARKS, PROCEDURES, MANEUVERS
DAY	NIGHT	CROSS-COUNTRY	ACTUAL INSTR.	SIMULATED INSTR.				
								I certify that the statements made by me on this form are true.
								PILOT'S SIGNATURE

YEAR 20___ DATE	AIRCRAFT MAKE & MODEL	AIRCRAFT IDENT.	POINTS OF DEPARTURE & ARRIVAL		AIRCRAFT CATEGORY						GROUND TRAINER		TYPE OF PILOTING TIME					
			FROM	TO	AIRPLANE SEL		AIRPLANE MEL						DUAL RECEIVED		PILOT-IN-COMMAND			
				PAGE TOTAL														
				AMOUNT FORWARD														
				TOTAL TO DATE														

CONDITIONS OF FLIGHT					NO. INSTR. APPR.	NO. LDG. DAY / NIGHT	TOTAL DURATION OF FLIGHT	REMARKS, PROCEDURES, MANEUVERS
DAY	NIGHT	CROSS-COUNTRY	ACTUAL INSTR.	SIMULATED INSTR.				

I certify that the statements made by me on this form are true.

PILOT'S SIGNATURE

YEAR 20___ DATE	AIRCRAFT MAKE & MODEL	AIRCRAFT IDENT.	POINTS OF DEPARTURE & ARRIVAL		AIRCRAFT CATEGORY			GROUND TRAINER	TYPE OF PILOTING TIME		
			FROM	TO	AIRPLANE **SEL**	AIRPLANE **MEL**			DUAL RECEIVED	PILOT-IN-COMMAND	
				PAGE TOTAL							
				AMOUNT FORWARD							
				TOTAL TO DATE							

CONDITIONS OF FLIGHT					NO. INSTR. APPR.	NO. LDG. DAY / NIGHT	TOTAL DURATION OF FLIGHT	REMARKS, PROCEDURES, MANEUVERS
DAY	NIGHT	CROSS-COUNTRY	ACTUAL INSTR.	SIMULATED INSTR.				
								I certify that the statements made by me on this form are true.
								PILOT'S SIGNATURE

YEAR 20___ DATE	AIRCRAFT MAKE & MODEL	AIRCRAFT IDENT.	POINTS OF DEPARTURE & ARRIVAL		AIRCRAFT CATEGORY			GROUND TRAINER	TYPE OF PILOTING TIME		
			FROM	TO	AIRPLANE **SEL**	AIRPLANE **MEL**			DUAL RECEIVED	PILOT-IN-COMMAND	
				PAGE TOTAL							
				AMOUNT FORWARD							
				TOTAL TO DATE							

CONDITIONS OF FLIGHT					NO. INSTR. APPR.	NO. LDG. DAY / NIGHT	TOTAL DURATION OF FLIGHT	REMARKS, PROCEDURES, MANEUVERS
DAY	NIGHT	CROSS-COUNTRY	ACTUAL INSTR.	SIMULATED INSTR.				

I certify that the statements made by me on this form are true.

PILOT'S SIGNATURE

YEAR 20___ DATE	AIRCRAFT MAKE & MODEL	AIRCRAFT IDENT.	POINTS OF DEPARTURE & ARRIVAL		AIRCRAFT CATEGORY								TYPE OF PILOTING TIME					
			FROM	TO	AIRPLANE **SEL**		AIRPLANE **MEL**				GROUND TRAINER		DUAL RECEIVED		PILOT-IN-COMMAND			
				PAGE TOTAL														
				AMOUNT FORWARD														
				TOTAL TO DATE														

CONDITIONS OF FLIGHT										NO. INSTR. APPR.	NO. LDG. DAY / NIGHT	TOTAL DURATION OF FLIGHT		REMARKS, PROCEDURES, MANEUVERS
DAY		NIGHT		CROSS-COUNTRY		ACTUAL INSTR.		SIMULATED INSTR.						

I certify that the statements made by me on this form are true.

PILOT'S SIGNATURE

GROUND INSTRUCTION LOG

DATE	LESSON PLAN	INSTRUCTOR	TIME	TOTAL

GROUND INSTRUCTION LOG

DATE	LESSON PLAN	INSTRUCTOR	TIME	TOTAL

YEAR 20____	CLASSIFICATION OF PILOT-IN-COMMAND TIME												
	JAN.	FEB.	MAR.	APR.	MAY	JUNE	JULY	AUG.	SEPT.	OCT.	NOV.	DEC.	TOTAL
SINGLE ENGINE													
MULTI-ENGINE													
TURBINE ENGINE													
CROSS-COUNTRY													
NIGHT													
GROUND TRAINER													
SIMULATED INSTRUMENT													
ACTUAL INSTRUMENT													
UNMANNED (UAS)													

YEAR 20____	CLASSIFICATION OF PILOT-IN-COMMAND TIME												
	JAN.	FEB.	MAR.	APR.	MAY	JUNE	JULY	AUG.	SEPT.	OCT.	NOV.	DEC.	TOTAL
SINGLE ENGINE													
MULTI-ENGINE													
TURBINE ENGINE													
CROSS-COUNTRY													
NIGHT													
GROUND TRAINER													
SIMULATED INSTRUMENT													
ACTUAL INSTRUMENT													
UNMANNED (UAS)													

AIRCRAFT FLOWN AND NUMBER OF HOURS IN EACH

AIRCRAFT MAKE AND MODEL	PIC	DUAL REC'D.	AIRCRAFT MAKE AND MODEL	PIC	DUAL REC'D.

INITIAL SOLO ENDORSEMENTS

I certify that *(First name, MI, Last name)* ________________________________, has satisfactorily completed the presolo knowledge exam of §61.87(b), received the required presolo training required by §61.87(c), and has demonstrated the proficiency of §61.87(d) and is proficient to make solo flights in *(category, make, model aircraft)* ________________________________.
SIGNED ________________________________ DATE ________________
INSTR. NO. ________________________________ RE/EXP. ________________

I certify that *(First name, MI, Last name)* ________________________________, has received the required training to qualify for local solo flying. I have determined he/she meets the applicable requirements of §61.87(n) and is proficient to make solo flights in *(category, make, model aircraft)* ________________ ________________ until *(maximum 90 days from date given)* ________________.
Limitations: ________________________________.
SIGNED ________________________________ DATE ________________
INSTR. NO. ________________________________ RE/EXP. ________________

ADDITIONAL AIRPORT WITHIN 25NM SOLO ENDORSEMENTS

I certify that *(First name, MI, Last name)* ________________________________, has received the required training of § 61.93(b)(1). I have determined that he/she is proficient to practice solo takeoffs and landings at *(airport name)* ________________________________ subject to the following conditions: ________________________________.
SIGNED ________________________________ DATE ________________
INSTR. NO. ________________________________ RE/EXP. ________________

I certify that *(First name, MI, Last name)* ________________________________, has received the required training of § 61.93(b)(1). I have determined that he/she is proficient to practice solo takeoffs and landings at *(airport name)* ________________________________ subject to the following conditions: ________________________________.
SIGNED ________________________________ DATE ________________
INSTR. NO. ________________________________ RE/EXP. ________________

CROSS-COUNTRY SOLO ENDORSEMENTS

I certify that *(First name, MI, Last name)* ________________________________, has received the required solo cross-country training and find he/she has met the applicable requirements of §61.93, and is proficient to make solo cross-country flights in a *(category, make, model aircraft)* ________________.
SIGNED ________________________________ DATE ________________
INSTR. NO. ________________________________ RE/EXP. ________________

I have reviewed the cross-country planning of *(First name, MI, Last name)* ________________ ________________ and find the planning and preparation to be correct to make the solo flight from *(location)* ________________ to *(destination)* ________________ via *(route of flight)* ________________ with landings at *(name the airports)* ________________ in a *(category, make, model aircraft)* ________________ on *(date)* ________________.
List any applicable conditions or limitations: ________________.
SIGNED ________________________________ DATE ________________
INSTR. NO. ________________________________ RE/EXP. ________________

ADDITIONAL SOLO ENDORSEMENTS

90-DAY SOLO (1ST 90-DAY PERIOD)

I certify that *(First name, MI, Last name)* ______________________________, has received the required training to qualify for local solo flying. I have determined he/she meets the applicable requirements of §61.87(n) and is proficient to make solo flights in *(category, make and model aircraft)* ________ ________________ until *(max 90 days from date given)* ____________.

Limitations: ______________________________.

SIGNED ______________________________ DATE ____________

INSTR. NO. ______________________________ RE/EXP. ____________

CLASS B SOLO

I certify that *(First name, MI, Last name)* ______________________________, has received the required training of §61.95(a) and determined he/she is proficient to conduct solo flights in *(name of Class B)* ______________ airspace. *List any applicable conditions or limitations:* ______________ ______________________________.

SIGNED ______________________________ DATE ____________

INSTR. NO. ______________________________ RE/EXP. ____________

90-DAY SOLO (ADDITIONAL 90-DAY PERIOD)

I certify that *(First name, MI, Last name)* ______________________________, has received the required training to qualify for local solo flying. I have determined he/she meets the applicable requirements of §61.87(p) and is proficient to make solo flights in *(category, make and model aircraft)* ________ ________________ until *(max 90 days from date given)* ____________.

Limitations: ______________________________.

SIGNED ______________________________ DATE ____________

INSTR. NO. ______________________________ RE/EXP. ____________

I certify that *(First name, MI, Last name)* ______________________________, has received the required training of §61.95(b)(1) and determined that he/she is proficient to conduct solo flight operations at *(name of airport)* ____________ ____________. *List any applicable conditions or limitations:* ____________ ______________________________.

SIGNED ______________________________ DATE ____________

INSTR. NO. ______________________________ RE/EXP. ____________

NIGHT SOLO

I certify that *(First name, MI, Last name)* ______________________________, has received the required presolo training in a *(category, make and model aircraft)* ________________ and determined he/she has demonstrated the proficiency of §61.87(o) and is proficient to make solo flights at night in a *(category, make and model aircraft)* ______________________________.

SIGNED ______________________________ DATE ____________

INSTR. NO. ______________________________ RE/EXP. ____________

REPEAT X/C SOLO (LESS THAN 50 NM)

I certify that *(First name, MI, Last name)* ______________________________, has received the required training in both directions between and at both *(airport names)*____________and determined that he/she is proficient in §61.93(b)(2) to conduct repeated solo cross-country flights over that route, which is not more than 50NM from the point of departure, subject to the following conditions: ______________________________.

SIGNED ______________________________ DATE ____________

INSTR. NO. ______________________________ RE/EXP. ____________

INITIAL SPORT PILOT ENDORSEMENTS

SOLO FLIGHT 1st 90-DAY

I certify that *(First name, MI, Last name)* ______________________________, has received the required training to qualify for local solo flying. I have determined he/she meets the applicable requirements of §61.87(n) and is proficient to make solo flights in *(make and model aircraft)* ______________ until *(maximum 90 days from date given)* ______________________.
Limitations: ____.

SIGNED ______________________________ DATE ______________
INSTR. NO. ____________________________ RE/EXP. ______________

SOLO FLIGHT IN CLASS B, C, AND D AIRSPACE (req. each add'l 90-day period)

I certify that *(First name, MI, Last name)* ______________________________, has received the required training of §61.94(a). I have determined he/she is proficient to conduct solo flights in *(name of Class B, C, or D)* ______ airspace.
List any applicable conditions or limitations: ______________________________
____.

SIGNED ______________________________ DATE ______________
INSTR. NO. ____________________________ RE/EXP. ______________

TAKING THE AERONAUTICAL KNOWLEDGE TEST

I certify that *(First name, MI, Last name)* ______________________________, has received the required aeronautical knowledge training of §61.309. I have determined that he/she is prepared for the *(name the knowledge test/aircraft category)* ____.

SIGNED ______________________________ DATE ______________
INSTR. NO. ____________________________ RE/EXP. ______________

TAKING THE SPORT PILOT PRACTICAL TEST

I certify that *(First name, MI, Last name)* ______________________________, has received the required training of §§61.309 and 61.311 and met the experience requirements of §61.313. I have determined that he/she is prepared for the *(category/class)* ______________________ practical test.

SIGNED ______________________________ DATE ______________
INSTR. NO. ____________________________ RE/EXP. ______________

I certify that *(First name, MI, Last name)* ______________________________, has received the required training and demonstrated satisfactory knowledge of deficient areas from the Sport Pilot knowledge test as required per §61.39 for the practical test.

SIGNED ______________________________ DATE ______________
INSTR. NO. ____________________________ RE/EXP. ______________

PASSING THE SPORT PILOT PRACTICAL TEST

I certify that *(First name, MI, Last name)* ______________________________, has met the training and endorsement requirements of §§61.309, 61.311 and 61.313. I have determined him/her proficient to act as PIC of *(category/class)* ______________________ of light-sport aircraft.

SIGNED ______________________________ DATE ______________
PILOT CERT # ______________ DPE # ________ EXP. DATE ______________

ADDITIONAL SPORT PILOT ENDORSEMENTS

TAKING FLIGHT PROFICIENCY CHECK FOR AN ADDITIONAL AIRCRAFT

I certify that *(First name, MI, Last name)* ____________________, has received the required training of §§61.309 and 61.311. I have determined that he/she is prepared for the *(category/class)* ____________ proficiency check.

SIGNED ____________________ DATE ____________

INSTR. NO. ____________________ RE/EXP. ____________

PASSING FLIGHT PROFICIENCY CHECK FOR AN ADDITIONAL AIRCRAFT

I certify that *(First name, MI, Last name)* ____________________, has met the training and endorsement requirements of §§61.309 and 61.311. I have determined him/her proficient to act as PIC of *(category/class)* ____________ of light-sport aircraft.

SIGNED ____________________ DATE ____________

INSTR. NO. ____________________ RE/EXP. ____________

PRIVILEGES TO OPERATE A DIFFERENT AIRCRAFT

I certify that *(First name, MI, Last name)* ____________________, has received the required training of §61.321 in a *(category/class)* ____________. I have determined him/her proficient to act as PIC of that light-sport aircraft.

SIGNED ____________________ DATE ____________

INSTR. NO. ____________________ RE/EXP. ____________

AIRSPACE & AIRSPEED ENDORSEMENTS

I certify that *(First name, MI, Last name)* ____________________, has received the required training of §61.327 in a *(make and model aircraft)* ____________. I have determined him/her proficient to act as PIC of a light-sport aircraft that has a V_H greater/less than 87 knots (kts) CAS.

SIGNED ____________________ DATE ____________

INSTR. NO. ____________________ RE/EXP. ____________

I certify that *(First name, MI, Last name)* ____________________, has received the required training of §61.325. I have determined he/she is proficient to conduct operations in Class B, C, or D airspace, at an airport located in Class B, C, or D airspace, or to, from, through, or on an airport having an operational control tower.

SIGNED ____________________ DATE ____________

INSTR. NO. ____________________ RE/EXP. ____________

I certify that *(First name, MI, Last name)* ____________________, has received the training required in accordance with §61.327 in a *(make and model aircraft)* . I have determined him/her proficient to act as PIC of a light-sport aircraft that has a V_H greater/less than 87 knots (kts) CAS.

SIGNED ____________________ DATE ____________

INSTR. NO. ____________________ RE/EXP. ____________

RECREATIONAL PILOT ENDORSEMENTS

I certify that *(First name, MI, Last name)* ______________________________, has received the required training of §61.97(b) and/or I have reviewed the home study curriculum and have determined that he/she is prepared for the *(name the knowledge test/aircraft category)* ______________________.

SIGNED ______________________ DATE ______________

INSTR. NO. ______________________ RE/EXP. ______________

I certify that *(First name, MI, Last name)* ______________________________, has received the required cross-country training of §61.101(c) and have determined that he/she is proficient in cross-country flying of part 61, subpart E.

SIGNED ______________________ DATE ______________

INSTR. NO. ______________________ RE/EXP. ______________

I certify that *(First name, MI, Last name)* ______________________________, has received the required training of §§61.98(b) and 61.99 and have determined that he/she is prepared for the *(name the practical test)* ______________________________.

SIGNED ______________________ DATE ______________

INSTR. NO. ______________________ RE/EXP. ______________

I certify that *(First name, MI, Last name)* ______________________________, has received the required 180-day recurrent training of §61.101(g) in a *(make and model aircraft)* ______________________. I have determined him/her to be proficient to act as PIC of that aircraft.

SIGNED ______________________ DATE ______________

INSTR. NO. ______________________ RE/EXP. ______________

I certify that *(First name, MI, Last name)* ______________________________, has received the required training of §61.101(b) and have determined he/she is competent to operate at the *(name of airport)* ______________________.

SIGNED ______________________ DATE ______________

INSTR. NO. ______________________ RE/EXP. ______________

I certify that *(First name, MI, Last name)* ______________________________, has received the required training of §61.87 in a *(make and model aircraft)* ______________________. I have determined he/she is prepared to conduct a solo flight on *(date) under the following conditions:* ______________________________.

SIGNED ______________________ DATE ______________

INSTR. NO. ______________________ RE/EXP. ______________

PRIVATE PILOT ENDORSEMENTS

I certify that *(First name, MI, Last name)* ______________________________, has received the required training of §61.105 and/or I have reviewed the home study curriculum and have determined he/she is prepared for the *(name the knowledge test/aircraft category)* ______________________________.

SIGNED ______________________________ DATE ______________

INSTR. NO. ______________________________ RE/EXP. ______________

I certify that *(First name, MI, Last name)* ______________________________, has received the required training of §§61.107 and 61.109 and have determined he/she is prepared for the *(name the practical test)* ______________________________

______________________________.

SIGNED ______________________________ DATE ______________

INSTR. NO. ______________________________ RE/EXP. ______________

I certify that *(First name, MI, Last name)* ______________________________, has received the training as required by §61.39(a)(6)(i) within the preceding two calendar months and have determined that he/she is prepared for the *(name the practical test)* ______________________________ and has demonstrated satisfactory knowledge of subject areas shown to be deficient on his/her Airman Knowledge Test as required by §61.39(a)(6)(iii).

SIGNED ______________________________ DATE ______________

INSTR. NO. ______________________________ RE/EXP. ______________

COMMERCIAL PILOT ENDORSEMENTS

I certify that *(First name, MI, Last name)* ______________________________, has received the required training of §61.125 and/or I have reviewed the home study curriculum and have determined that he/she is prepared for the *(name the knowledge test/aircraft category)* ______________________________.

SIGNED ______________________________ DATE ______________

INSTR. NO. ______________________________ RE/EXP. ______________

I certify that *(First name, MI, Last name)* ______________________________, has received the required training of §§61.127 and 61.129 and have determined he/she is prepared for the *(name the practical test)* ______________________________

______________________________.

SIGNED ______________________________ DATE ______________

INSTR. NO. ______________________________ RE/EXP. ______________

I certify that *(First name, MI, Last name)* ______________________________, has received the training as required by §61.39(a)(6)(i) within the preceding two calendar months and have determined that he/she is prepared for the *(name the practical test)* ______________________________ and has demonstrated satisfactory knowledge of subject areas shown to be deficient on his/her Airman Knowledge Test as required by §61.39(a)(6)(iii).

SIGNED ______________________________ DATE ______________

INSTR. NO. ______________________________ RE/EXP. ______________

INSTRUMENT RATING ENDORSEMENTS	INSTRUMENT PROFICIENCY
I certify that *(First name, MI, Last name)* ______________________, has received the required training of §61.65(b) and/or I have reviewed the home study curriculum and have determined that he/she is prepared for the *(name the knowledge test/aircraft category)* ______________. SIGNED ____________________ DATE __________ INSTR. NO. ____________________ RE/EXP. __________	I certify that *(First name, MI, Last name)* ______________________, *(pilot certificate)* ______________, *(certificate number)* __________, has satisfactorily completed the instrument proficiency check required in §61.57(d) in a *(make and model of aircraft)* ______________ on *(date)* __________. SIGNED ____________________ DATE __________ INSTR. NO. ____________________ RE/EXP. __________
I certify that *(First name, MI, Last name)* ______________________, has received the required training of §61.65(c) and (d) and have determined he/she is prepared for the *(name of the practical test)* ______________ ______________. SIGNED ____________________ DATE __________ INSTR. NO. ____________________ RE/EXP. __________	I certify that *(First name, MI, Last name)* ______________________, *(pilot certificate)* ______________, *(certificate number)* __________, has satisfactorily completed the instrument proficiency check required in §61.57(d) in a *(make and model of aircraft)* ______________ on *(date)* __________. SIGNED ____________________ DATE __________ INSTR. NO. ____________________ RE/EXP. __________
I certify that *(First name, MI, Last name)* ______________________, has received the training as required by §61.39(a)(6)(i) within the preceding two calendar months and have determined that he/she is prepared for the *(name the practical test)* ______________ and has demonstrated satisfactory knowledge of subject areas shown to be deficient on his/her Airman Knowledge Test as required by §61.39(a)(6)(iii). SIGNED ____________________ DATE __________ INSTR. NO. ____________________ RE/EXP. __________	I certify that *(First name, MI, Last name)* ______________________, *(pilot certificate)* ______________, *(certificate number)* __________, has satisfactorily completed the instrument proficiency check required in §61.57(d) in a *(make and model of aircraft)* ______________ on *(date)* __________. SIGNED ____________________ DATE __________ INSTR. NO. ____________________ RE/EXP. __________

FLIGHT AND GROUND INSTRUCTOR ENDORSEMENTS

I certify that *(First name, MI, Last name)* ________________________________,
has received the required fundamentals of instruction training of §61.185(a)(1).

SIGNED ________________________________ DATE ____________
INSTR. NO. ____________________________ RE/EXP. ____________

I certify that *(First name, MI, Last name)* ________________________________
has received the required training of §61.183(i) and have determined that he/she is competent and proficient in instructional skills for training stall awareness, spin entry, spins, and spin recovery procedures. *(Required of flight instructor applicants for the airplane and glider ratings only.)*

SIGNED ________________________________ DATE ____________
INSTR. NO. ____________________________ RE/EXP. ____________

I certify that *(First name, MI, Last name)* ________________________________,
has received the required training of §61.187(b) and/or I have reviewed the home study curriculum and have determined he/she is prepared for the *(name the knowledge test/aircraft category)* ________________________________.

SIGNED ________________________________ DATE ____________
INSTR. NO. ____________________________ RE/EXP. ____________

I certify that *(First name, MI, Last name)* ________________________________
has demonstrated satisfactory proficiency on the appropriate ground instructor knowledge and training subjects of §61.213(a)(3) and (a)(4).

SIGNED ________________________________ DATE ____________
INSTR. NO. ____________________________ RE/EXP. ____________

I certify that *(First name, MI, Last name)* ________________________________,
has received the required CFII training of §61.187(b)(7) and have determined he/she is prepared for the *(name of practical test)* ________________________________
________________________________.

SIGNED ________________________________ DATE ____________
INSTR. NO. ____________________________ RE/EXP. ____________

I certify that *(First name, MI, Last name)* ________________________________,
has received the training as required by §61.39(a)(6)(i) within the preceding two calendar months and have determined that he/she is prepared for the *(name the practical test)* ________________________________
and has demonstrated satisfactory knowledge of subject areas shown to be deficient on his/her Airman Knowledge Test as required by §61.39(a)(6)(iii).

SIGNED ________________________________ DATE ____________
INSTR. NO. ____________________________ RE/EXP. ____________

ADDITIONAL ENDORSEMENTS

COMPLEX AIRPLANE

I certify that *(First name, MI, Last name)* ____________________, *(pilot certificate)* ____________, *(certificate number)* ____________, has received the required training of §61.31(e) in a *(make and model of complex airplane)* ____________________. I have determined that he/she is proficient in the operation and systems of a complex airplane.

SIGNED ____________________ DATE ____________

INSTR. NO. ____________________ RE/EXP. ____________

TAILWHEEL

I certify that *(First name, MI, Last name)* ____________________, *(pilot certificate)* ____________, *(certificate number)* ____________, has received the required training of §61.31(i) in a *(make and model of tailwheel airplane)* ____________________. I have determined that he/she is proficient in the operation of a tailwheel airplane.

SIGNED ____________________ DATE ____________

INSTR. NO. ____________________ RE/EXP. ____________

HIGH-PERFORMANCE AIRPLANE

I certify that *(First name, MI, Last name)* ____________________, *(pilot certificate)* ____________, *(certificate number)* ____________, has received the required training of §61.31(f) in a *(make and model of high performance airplane)* ____________________. I have determined that he/she is proficient in the operation and systems of a high performance airplane.

SIGNED ____________________ DATE ____________

INSTR. NO. ____________________ RE/EXP. ____________

TYPE RATING

I certify that *(First name, MI, Last name)* ____________________, has received the training as required by §61.31(d)(2) to serve as a PIC in a *(category and class of aircraft)* ____________________. I have determined that he/she is prepared to serve as PIC in that *(make and model of aircraft)* ____________________.

SIGNED ____________________ DATE ____________

INSTR. NO. ____________________ RE/EXP. ____________

HIGH ALTITUDE

I certify that *(First name, MI, Last name)* ____________________, *(pilot certificate)* ____________, *(certificate number)* ____________, has received the required training of §61.31(g) in a *(make and model of pressurized aircraft)* ____________________. I have determined that he/she is proficient in the operation and systems of a pressurized aircraft.

SIGNED ____________________ DATE ____________

INSTR. NO. ____________________ RE/EXP. ____________

ADDED RATING

I certify that *(First name, MI, Last name)* ____________________, *(pilot certificate)* ____________, *(certificate number)* ____________, has received the required training for an additional *(name the aircraft category/class rating)* ____________________. I have determined that he/she is prepared for the *(name the practical test)* ____________________ for the addition of a *(name the aircraft category/class rating)* ____________________.

SIGNED ____________________ DATE ____________

INSTR. NO. ____________________ RE/EXP. ____________

FLIGHT REVIEW

I certify that *(First name, MI, Last name)* ______________________________,
(pilot certificate) ____________________, *(certificate number)* ______________,
has satisfactorily completed the flight review required in §61.56(a) on *(date)*
______________________.

SIGNED ______________________________ DATE ______________

INSTR. NO. ______________________________ RE/EXP. ______________

I certify that *(First name, MI, Last name)* ______________________________,
(pilot certificate) ____________________, *(certificate number)* ______________,
has satisfactorily completed the flight review required in §61.56(a) on *(date)*
______________________.

SIGNED ______________________________ DATE ______________

INSTR. NO. ______________________________ RE/EXP. ______________

I certify that *(First name, MI, Last name)* ______________________________,
(pilot certificate) ____________________, *(certificate number)* ______________,
has satisfactorily completed the flight review required in §61.56(a) on *(date)*
______________________.

SIGNED ______________________________ DATE ______________

INSTR. NO. ______________________________ RE/EXP. ______________

I certify that *(First name, MI, Last name)* ______________________________,
(pilot certificate) ____________________, *(certificate number)* ______________,
has satisfactorily completed the flight review required in §61.56(a) on *(date)*
______________________.

SIGNED ______________________________ DATE ______________

INSTR. NO. ______________________________ RE/EXP. ______________

I certify that *(First name, MI, Last name)* ______________________________,
(pilot certificate) ____________________, *(certificate number)* ______________,
has satisfactorily completed the flight review required in §61.56(a) on *(date)*
______________________.

SIGNED ______________________________ DATE ______________

INSTR. NO. ______________________________ RE/EXP. ______________

I certify that *(First name, MI, Last name)* ______________________________,
(pilot certificate) ____________________, *(certificate number)* ______________,
has satisfactorily completed the flight review required in §61.56(a) on *(date)*
______________________.

SIGNED ______________________________ DATE ______________

INSTR. NO. ______________________________ RE/EXP. ______________